Ipswich
in the '50s & '60s

at heart ♡ publications

EveningStar

First published in 2006 by: At Heart Publications,
32 Stamford Street, Altrincham, Cheshire, WA14 1EY
in conjunction with Evening Star, Ipswich, Suffolk.

Images and text: ©2006 Evening Star unless otherwise stated.

ISBN: 1-84547-102-4

Ipswich
in the '50s & '60s

Contents

Acknowledgements

My thanks to everybody who has helped with this project including the staff at the Suffolk Record Office who traced many of the photographs taken by the East Anglian Daily Times and Evening Star, which was deposited with them when the company moved from Carr Street in 1966.

To Colin Barber for the Speedway photographs from the 1950s and to my wife Anne who supplies the tea and sympathy as I try to trace names and dates for photographs taken up to half a century ago.

David Kindred

Introduction

As the 1950s began, the country was just starting to recover from the Second World War. There were still many shortages and some rationing for food, but there was optimism in the air. Like everybody else, Ipswich people were looking for some good news and were ready for change.

Sporting history was made in this period by Ipswich Town Football Club as they rose from being in the backwaters to winning the Division One title with manager Alf Ramsey. The 1960s came to an end with the arrival of another legend, Bobby Robson.

Foxhall Stadium was built on the edge of Ipswich when speedway came to town. The Witches had their first match in 1951. The timing was perfect with people hungry for some excitement and entertainment within reach of home when few families could afford a car. Huge crowds flocked to the stadium every Thursday evening in the early Fifties.

The baby boom after the Second World War brought a new teenage culture in the early Sixties with the arrival of rock and pop music. Ipswich was well served with all the big names coming to town; The Beatles shows in '63 and '64 saw a great rush for tickets, as did all the other top names performing at the Gaumont.

For just a few shillings The Jazz Club brought the top names in 'Trad' Jazz and later it became Bluesville with rhythm and blues. There was also a very active local band line up with several gigs a week for teenagers to attend.

It was an era when parades and carnivals attracted huge crowds. The Co-op Fete in Christchurch Park saw crowds of over 20,000.

Town planners saw the period as a time for change. Sadly, not all the changes were wise ones. 'The Potteries' around Rope Walk was cleared in the 1930s, as was the housing around Cox Lane between Carr Street and Tacket Street. Residents had been moved to the new council estates on the edge of town. Unfortunately, the good was destroyed with the bad and some very old and fine buildings were demolished along with the slums.

The war years saw a complete halt to redevelopment, but as the 1950s progressed, builders started on the Civic College at the former Potteries site. The college was formally opened by the Queen in 1961. The Cox Lane area is still a car park.

The Mount area of town was demolished in the Fifties as plans were set in motion to cut a dual carriageway road through from St Matthew's Street, on the west side of town, to take traffic to the east side. This was all planned long before the Orwell Bridge was on the drawing board.

The new road completed in the mid Sixties came to a strange end at right angles to the narrow St Nicholas Street. Many years later, Franciscan Way became Cromwell Square car park and the road was diverted to a roundabout system near St Peter's Church.

Old shops and a seventeenth century hotel in St Matthew's Street were torn down and ugly units, built further back to widen the road, took their place. Greyfriars was built where back-to-back houses and shops stood around Princes Street.

The chimney at St Matthew's Baths was being demolished in January 1965, as what was to become Civic Drive was just a sea of mud. The huge hole that was being dug to create the underground car park is top left.

This was an ill-fated '60s concept that most hated. Planners thought they could move the shopping centre to Greyfriars, but it stood largely empty for twenty years before being restructured.

In Carr Street, the fine red brick Victorian building, which was home to the East Anglian Daily Times Company, and the buildings all around were demolished in 1967 and a grey concrete shopping centre built in their place. The heart of this old street was torn out in a few weeks.

Ipswich was lucky not to suffer too many tower blocks in the changes of this era, and now many of the mistakes made in the '50s and '60s have been rectified. The Greyfriars scheme was reshaped in the mid 1980s and is now, apart from St Francis Tower, mainly used as offices. In Great Colman Street, part of what was built as Carr Precinct was also demolished and red brick buildings, more sympathetic to the surrounding area, were constructed. The mistakes made in the 1960s were in many cases like "a monstrous carbuncle on the face of a much-loved and elegant friend," as Prince Charles said of plans to build an extension of London's National Gallery in 1984. The Prince went on, "Why can't we have those curves and arches that express feeling in design? What is wrong with them? Why has everything got to be vertical, straight, unbending, only at right angles and functional?"

What a pity he was not old enough to challenge the plans to rebuild parts of Ipswich in square concrete blocks in the 1950s and '60s.

David Kindred 2006.

Around Ipswich

The 1950s and 1960s was a time of huge change for Ipswich. Plans were made during the 1950s to modernise the town. Planners foresaw the huge increase in traffic the town would face in the 1960s and beyond, so a dual carriageway to take traffic across town from St Matthew's Street to the east side was on the drawing board.

Work started in the 1950s to clear the houses round The Mount area of town between St Matthew's Street and Elm Street. Residents were moved to council housing out of the town centre.

When the road was completed in the mid 1960s it came to a sudden end with the ancient and narrow St Nicholas Street across its path with plans to cut through to the Fore Street side of town never materialising.

In the 1960s housing and businesses in the area around Princes Street were demolished to build shops, offices, a car park and a tower block of modern flats. This was the ill-fated Greyfriars scheme, which was shunned by businesses with very few of the shopping units ever being occupied before much of the site was demolished in 1984.

Old shops were knocked down in St Matthew's Street and part of Crown Street to create a few hundred yards of dual carriageway with single carriageway roads at each end.

In Carr Street the pleasing red brick Victorian building, then home to the East Anglian Daily Times Company, and other similar buildings, were demolished to create space for the grey concrete structure of Carr Precinct.

Sadly, much of the old town was destroyed in just a few years. In this chapter we will see how our ancient town was changed forever in that twenty year period.

The Cornhill in 1956 with trolley buses at the bus stops. In the background is Grimwade's store at the corner of Westgate Street. On the right of Westgate Street is Footman's Waterloo House store, now the site of Debenhams. The Lloyds Avenue arch is on the right. The Cornhill is now closed to through traffic.

The Cornhill from the Town Hall in 1951. Traffic at the junction of Lloyds Avenue, Princes Street and Tavern Street was then controlled by a policeman. Drivers were able to park in the streets and in front of the Town Hall.

Workmen perched on the roof of the Town Hall removing decorative work which has become unsafe. They are working above Princes Street with the Cornhill in the background.

The Christmas lights on the Cornhill in 1964. The Christmas display then had to compete with bus stops and parked cars.

Around Ipswich

The Old Cattle Market in the mid 1960s. On the left is the Blue Coat Boy public house. At the junction with Silent Street there were underground public toilets. The new St Francis Tower at Greyfriars is in the background.

The Old Cattle Market Post Office sorting office, which was situated opposite the Blue Coat Boy public house. This building was demolished when the sorting office moved to the junction of Princes Street and Grafton Way. Part of the Buttermarket Shopping Centre is now on this site.

A busy day at the Corn Exchange in February 1957. Corn dealers traded here regularly. The foundation stone was laid on October 22, 1880 and the building opened in 1882. It was also home to the Ipswich produce market (pictured right in 1969) until it was moved to the new Greyfriars site in 1970. An upper floor was added to the building when it was converted to an entertainment complex, which was formally opened by the Duke of Gloucester in September 1975.

The popular produce market in the Corn Exchange as it was in August 1969.

A trolley bus in Westgate Street in the mid 1950s, travelling from the Cornhill towards St Matthew's Street. Shoppers were then able to park in the street and leave their bicycles at the kerb. On the left of the street are: The Fifty Shilling Tailors, Stone's radio shop, The Crown and Anchor Hotel and Footman's Waterloo House store. Included on the right are: The Oriental Café and W. H. Smith and Son stationers.

Westgate Street from the junction with High Street in the mid '50s. Included on the right of the street are Leaman's, Dorothy Perkins and Burney's ladies' fashion shops, the Singer Sewing Machine Company, Janus Ltd ladies' outfitters and G.A. Dunn and Company hatters. The entrance to the Public Hall is halfway along the street on the right. This was badly damaged by fire in 1948 and stood closed for several years.

The Christmas lights in Westgate Street in 1964. The red and white stars hung over the street which was then open to traffic. This view was taken from outside the Crown and Anchor Hotel looking towards High Street.

Westgate Street from Lloyds Avenue around 1950 as a policeman helps children to cross the busy road.

A popular feature at Christmas time in the Footman's store was the rides at Santa's Grotto. The basement area was cleared of paint and wallpaper stock to create a fantasy fun-world for young visitors.

Footman's store in the town centre was one of the biggest in town and at Christmas time thousands of children would visit with their parents to see Father Christmas. This photograph was taken at Tower Ramparts in the 1950s as Father Christmas arrived.

The baker's shop in Footman's town centre store. Debenhams now occupies this site.

The Lloyds Avenue entrance to Footman's Waterloo House store in the mid 1960s.

The food department at Footman's store was just inside the Lloyds Avenue entrance. Shoppers would be greeted with the aroma of cheese, roast coffee and freshly baked bread.

Top left: This rather ugly building at Major's Corner was demolished in the 1960s not long after this photograph was taken. Avis Cook's television and radio shop was at the corner of Old Foundry Road with Sarony's photographers situated in the centre. The shoe repair shop and Ipswich Travel House had already closed. Carr Street is off to the left.

Left: Carr Street was redeveloped in the mid 1960s and all of the buildings from Little Colman Street to the Co-op store on the right of this view were demolished. The building in the centre was used by Eastern Gas in 1967 as a temporary showroom while their new premises were being built in the new shopping precinct.

Top right: The Eastern Gas showrooms in Carr Street were originally home to the Ipswich Gas Light Company before the industry was nationalised. The workshops for the gas fitters were behind the showrooms with access from Old Foundry Road. These buildings were all demolished when the concrete Carr Precinct was built.

The composing room at the East Anglian Daily Times Company in the 1950s. Type was set on the Linotype machines on the left and pages made up on 'the stone' on the right.

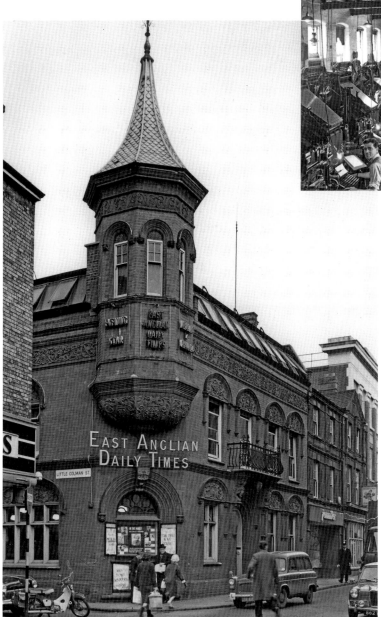

The fleet of vans belonging to the East Anglian Daily Times Company parked beside the building in Little Colman Street in 1965. The printing press was in the back half of the building and the huge reels of newsprint were stored in sheds on the left of the street.

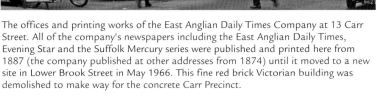

The offices and printing works of the East Anglian Daily Times Company at 13 Carr Street. All of the company's newspapers including the East Anglian Daily Times, Evening Star and the Suffolk Mercury series were published and printed here from 1887 (the company published at other addresses from 1874) until it moved to a new site in Lower Brook Street in May 1966. This fine red brick Victorian building was demolished to make way for the concrete Carr Precinct.

Tavern Street from Carr Street in the
1950s. The Great White Horse Hotel is on
the right. Opposite the hotel is Croydon's
the jewellers. Halfway along the street on
the right is J and J Edwards clothes shop
where thousands of schoolchildren were
taken to buy their uniforms. At the corner
of Upper Brook Street (left) is Berners
ladies clothes shop.

Upper Brook Street in January 1965. The
buildings featured have changed very little
in over forty years although few of the
businesses remain. Among those featured
on the right of the street are: Millett's
outfitters, Raper Victor gents' outfitters,
W. Turner's boot store, Dors fashions,
Madame Baldwin milliner and
Thompson's estate agents.

The Picture House Cinema and restaurant in Tavern Street. It closed in 1958 and was demolished the following year. A Timothy White's store was built on the site, which is now a branch of Boots.

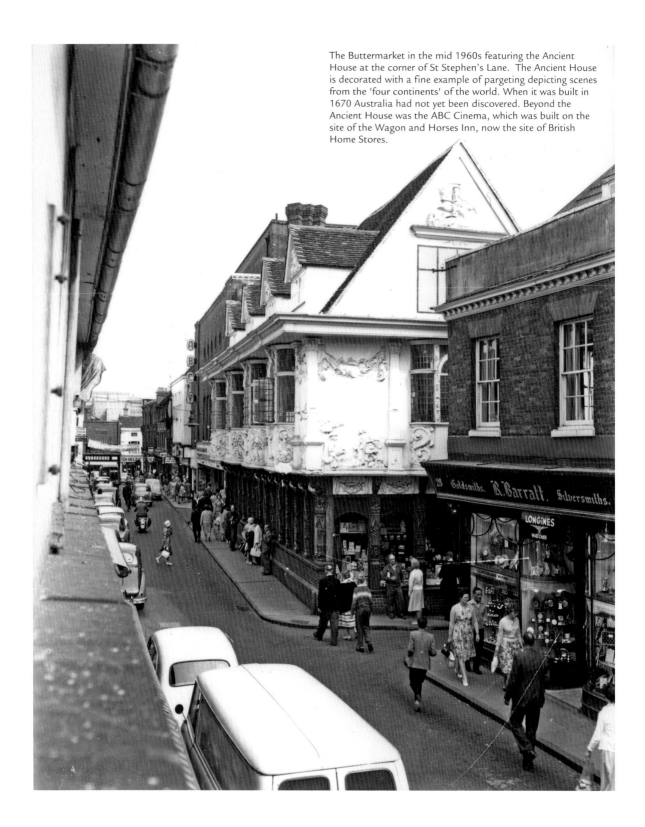

The Buttermarket in the mid 1960s featuring the Ancient House at the corner of St Stephen's Lane. The Ancient House is decorated with a fine example of pargeting depicting scenes from the 'four continents' of the world. When it was built in 1670 Australia had not yet been discovered. Beyond the Ancient House was the ABC Cinema, which was built on the site of the Wagon and Horses Inn, now the site of British Home Stores.

The Buttermarket from near the Ancient House in January 1965. Parking was then allowed in the street. The shops from St Stephen's Lane were R. Barratt jewellers, A. H. Croasdale Limited chemists, Murdoch's record and electrical appliance dealers, Madam Crow ladies hairdressers, James Parnell boot and shoe shop, A. J. Rawlings opticians, Limmer and Pipe provisions and restaurant and Cowells department store.

Below is the opposite view of the Buttermarket, taken in January 1965. Cowells store was demolished when the Buttermarket Shopping Centre, which opened in 1992, was built.

The centre of Ipswich from high above St
Helen's Street in 1964. In the centre is St
Mary-le-Tower Church. Carr Street, Tavern
Street, and Westgate Street run from the
bottom of the photograph. Egerton's huge
garage in Crown Street (see page 25), now
home to Crown Pools, is just to the right
of centre. All of the housing around
Charles Street, behind the garage, was
demolished in 1966.

Great Colman Street from the junction of Old Foundry Road in 1965. The premises of Rands and Jeckell Ltd marquee and tent manufacturers, on the left, were demolished in 1967 when the site was cleared and Carr Precinct built.

Great Colman Street from Old Foundry Road, looking towards the junction with Woodbridge Road. The Royal Air Forces Association were then located in the former Marquis Cornwallis public house.

Great Colman Street looking towards Northgate Street in 1965. The building, then occupied by Sketchley Cleaners, opened in 1821 as the Assembly Rooms. It later became the Ipswich High School for girls, which is now located at Woolverstone. The tower and spire of St Mary-le-Tower Church is just visible in the background.

A traffic survey in London Road in July 1963. This is now one of the busiest junctions in town where London Road meets West End Road (left) and Yarmouth Road (right).

The brick Seven Arches Bridge across the River Orwell on London Road was about to be demolished and a new stronger bridge built to take the increase in traffic when this photograph was taken in April 1959. The buildings at the corner of West End Road, featured from the opposite side in the picture above, are in the background.

All of the buildings featured in this photograph of Crown Street from June 1959 have since been demolished. The houses on the left were between Fitzroy Street and Chenery Street. Egerton's Garage is in the background. The building on the right was the premises of William Pretty's clothing manufacturers.

Egerton's garage dominated the Tower Ramparts area of Ipswich until it was demolished in the 1970s. The market site was here for a few years until work started on Crown Pools.
The Cricketers public house is on the right. The car park in the foreground was created in the 1930s when houses and shops on the site were demolished. It is now the town bus station. This photograph was taken around 1966.

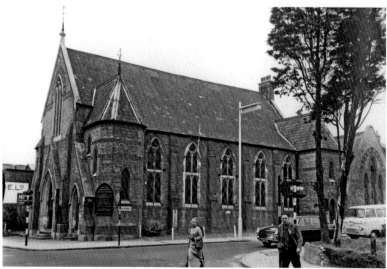

Above: Crown Street in the mid 1960s. On the left is St Matthew's Street. The shops from St George's Street included Aldridge's sports outfitters, Ipswich Flooring Service, Newsteads bakery, S. B. Blumfield confectioners, and Vera Dunningham ladies hairdressers.

Top left: W. J. Coe's garage in Crown Street. The site had been sold when this photograph was taken in the late 1960s. On the right is the Crown Street Congregational Church at the corner of High Street.

Left: The Crown Street Congregational Church at the junction of High Street (right) and Crown Street in 1965. All of the buildings featured on this page were demolished and the road widened. Offices now front all of these sites.

The Crown Iron Works of George Abbott Limited at the corner of High Street (left) and Crown Street in October 1963. The building, which was built in 1840, as the Temperance Hall, was demolished in the mid 1960s. An office block now stands on the site.

Peel Street looking towards Crown Street in November 1965. The following year all of these houses were demolished. A multi-storey car park now stands on this site. The building in the background was the premises of William Pretty's clothing manufacturers.

A view from the William Pretty factory as the streets of terraced houses off Crown Street were being demolished in August 1966. Most of the houses of Beck Street, Charles Street, Fitzroy Street, Peel Street, Chenery Street, Navarre Street and William Street were also cleared and replaced by offices and a multi-storey car park.

The demolition of houses in Beck Street in August 1966.

Tacket Street in August 1958. All of these buildings, including the Salvation Army Citadel and the Tankard public house, have been demolished and the road widened.

The Anglesea Road Wing of the Ipswich and East Suffolk Hospital from Berners Street in March 1967. The hospital opened on this site in 1836. The building originally had only two storeys but a third was added in 1869. The hospital site expanded over a large area until all services were moved to Heath Road and most of the site demolished in 1988. The original Victorian building, with its entrance between four columns, is now a nursing home.

Ipswich in the '50s & '60s

Ipswich from the air around 1950. This aerial view from above Stoke Hill has the junction of Princes Street and Portman Road in the bottom left-hand corner. In the bottom right corner is St Peter's Church with Christchurch Park in the top centre and Cardinal Park in the foreground.

Ipswich in the '50s & '60s

Princes Street in September 1960. All of the buildings featured in this photograph looking towards the town centre have been demolished. The Civic Drive roundabout now stands in the centre of the street. Off to the right is Portman Street with the Friars Inn on the corner and on the right is Latimer's Garage. The Greyfriars development was built to the right of this view.

The Princes Street area was prone to flooding. This photograph was taken during a summer downpour in July 1963, which thankfully caused only minor problems. This low lying part of town was badly hit and hundreds of homes ruined after heavy rain and melting snow flooded the area by several feet deep when the river burst its banks in 1939.

Buildings being demolished in Princes Street at the junction of Curriers Lane and Tanners Lane (background) in February. The Princes Street Civic Drive roundabout is now located where the men are working.

Workmen building the Princes Street Civic Drive roundabout in February 1965 as St Francis Tower, part of the Greyfriars scheme, takes shape in the background. The British Lion public house stands behind the workmen.

Giant cranes over St Francis Tower at the Greyfriars development in January 1965. The buildings in the foreground awaiting demolition include Spurling and Hempson sale yard for cattle, sheep and swine, Latimer's garage and the terraced houses of Portman Street.

A view through the partly demolished buildings of Princes Street towards the construction of St Francis Tower, part of the Greyfriars development, in February 1965.

Spurling and Hempson sale yard off Princes Street in 1962.

Cattle being unloaded from rail trucks in the 1950s in the days when the town hosted weekly cattle markets on sites around Princes Street. Animals were herded along the street to and from pens at sidings near the Princes Street bridge. Residents of nearby streets would often find cattle and pigs outside their front doors or sometimes inside their homes on market days!

The view from St Francis Tower in 1965 as Civic Drive was being cut
through St Matthew's Street. In the bottom right corner is the British Lion
public house, as featured on page 33. The shape of the Princes Street
roundabout was being formed in the foreground.

Onlookers gather outside E.L. Reeve's
newsagency as elephants from
Chipperfield's Circus parade along Princes
Street in October 1961. The animals had
arrived at Ipswich Station and were on
their way to Christchurch Park where the
circus was sited.

Princes Street, February 22, 1950. A huge fire destroyed these premises causing around £100,000 worth of damage. The fires started in the premises of Haddock and Baines paper merchants and printers and spread to the Central Cinema next door. The junction of the Buttermarket can be seen in the background.

A car park was built off Lady Lane in the 1950s when houses in Castle Street, Stirling Street, Perth Street and St Matthew's Church Lane were demolished. The area was redeveloped in the mid 1960s and the Civic Centre now stands where the streets of tiny terraced houses once stood. This photograph was taken in Lady Lane in September 1964.

Houses in Lady Lane being demolished in September 1964.

The Mount area of Ipswich from the air around 1960. The Lady
Lane car park featured on page 38 is top centre, with St
Matthew's Church in the top left corner. Civic Drive now runs
from top left to bottom right. The Ipswich Town Football Club
ground in Portman Road is in the bottom left corner.

Streets of small houses close to the
Ipswich town centre were demolished in
December 1958. The area known as
The Mount is where Civic Drive, the
police station and Wolsey Theatre and
Civic Centre are now. Among the streets
to disappear from the map were St
Matthew's Church Lane (pictured),
Castle Street, Mount Street, Perth Street
and Stirling Street. In the left background
is the glass roof and chimney at St
Matthew's Baths.

A cold winter's day in Elm Street in February 1956. This view was taken from what is now the entrance to the police station car park. The tower of St Mary at the Elms Church is in the background.

Youngsters make their way home in the snow along Elm Street in February 1956. St Mary at the Elms Church is on the right.

The new Civic Drive taking traffic from Princes Street (across the bottom of the picture) and St Matthew's Street was open to traffic when this aerial view was taken in June 1966. Work had started on the site of the Civic Centre and police station at the junction with Elm Street. The Greyfriars development is in the foreground.

The huge hole in the foreground of this
aerial view taken in 1965 was dug out to
create the underground car park in Civic
Drive. The line of Civic Drive runs to the
Greyfriars development. The dock is just
visible in the top left corner.

The underground spiral car park in Civic
Drive under construction. The Wolsey
Theatre is now in the top of this view.

Most of the shops on the north side of St Matthew's Street were demolished to widen the road in the mid 1960s. This view was taken around 1960 from the corner of St Matthew's Church Lane looking towards Westgate Street. The Queen's Head public house is on the right.

St Matthew's Street from the junction with Crown Street and Westgate Street in December 1963. All of the buildings featured on the right were demolished to create a dual carriageway. The building on the extreme right was the Rainbow public house at the corner of St George's Street.

Crown Street (left) and Westgate Street from St Matthew's Street in January 1956. Traffic was controlled at this junction by a police officer. The two policemen in the centre were about to change shifts.

St Matthew's Street from the junction with Westgate Street and Crown Street in December 1966.

St Matthew's Street in November 1962. All the buildings from the right of this view to the Golden Fleece Hotel were to be demolished to widen the road. Only the pair of shops on the extreme left are still standing to this day. The studios of BBC Radio Suffolk are now situated behind these shops.

The Golden Fleece Hotel was one of the first buildings in St Matthew's Street to be demolished. The entrance to Berners Street is behind the car towing the trailer. The Civic Drive roundabout now stands here.

St Matthew's Street from Crown Street in 1956. On the right is the Rainbow public house at the corner of St George's Street.

St Matthew's Baths Hall served as one of the town's two indoor swimming pools until it was replaced by Crown Pools, which was officially opened by the Mayor Peter Gardiner in May 1984. The hall was also used as a venue for meetings, wrestling matches, exhibitions and music events during the winter months when the pool was boarded over.

Whitelaw's store in St Matthew's Street was badly damaged by fire in October 1963.

St Matthew's Street in February 1956 as cables were laid to the new telephone exchange in Portman Road. The Queen's Head public house in the background was at the corner of St Matthew's Church Lane. Civic Drive now joins St Matthew's Street here.

The landlord and landlady of The Queen's Head public house in St Matthew's Street with some of their regulars in December 1963, shortly before the pub closed for demolition.

The Hippodrome Theatre in St Nicholas Street in April 1955. The theatre was built in 1905 as a variety and music hall. In the 1930s it operated as a cinema returning to live shows in 1941. It was converted to the Savoy Ballroom in 1957 and later became a bingo hall before being demolished in 1985. Offices now stand on the site.

Australian acrobat, Eddie Ash, performing a publicity stunt on the parapet of the Hippodrome Theatre high above St Nicholas Street in the 1950s.

Workmen were painting the Hippodrome Theatre when this picture was taken of St Nicholas Street in the early 1950s. St Peter's Church at the end of St Peter's Street can be seen in the background.

These buildings opposite the Half Moon Inn (pictured below) at the corner of Lower Brook Street and Foundation Street were demolished in the early 1960s. A car park belonging to Archant, publishers of the East Anglian Daily Times and Evening Star, now occupies this site.

The timber framed building of The Half Moon Inn at the junction of Lower Brook Street and Foundation Street was demolished in 1959 soon after this photograph was taken. The house just in view on the extreme left is featured in the photograph above.

The buildings at the Tacket Street end of Foundation Street were on the list for demolition when these photographs were taken in the 1950s. Only the building on the extreme right at the corner of Tacket Street is still standing in this view looking towards the dock.

This building at the corner of Little Wingfield Street was known as Felaw's House; it was left to Ipswich grammar school in the will of Richard Felaw, a wealthy local merchant, around 1482. Richard Felaw was bailiff of Ipswich eight times and represented Ipswich at Parliament twice. The buildings were demolished in 1963. A multi storey car park now stands on this site.

The buildings either side of Wingfield Street were included in the clearance of Foundation Street. Silos at the dock, which were demolished in 2006, are just visible in the distance.

Foundation Street at the junction of Star Lane (left) and Turret Lane in the 1950s. St Mary at the Quay Church, with its 73 foot tower, was then topped by a wooden cupola containing a sanctus bell. Other than the church all of the buildings between the camera and College Street have been demolished and Star Lane is now a busy one way road from St Peter's Church carrying one way traffic through to Grimwade Street. In the background is Cranfield's Mill in College Street. The silo on the left, behind the church, was demolished in 2006.

A view from a silo at Ipswich dock taken in the late 1950s. In the centre is St Mary at the Quay Church. The buildings to the left of the church tower stood where Star Lane now cuts through to Fore Street and on to Grimwade Street. In the left foreground is the Sea Horse public house. The tower of St Clement's Church is in the top right corner.

Ipswich in the '50s & '60s

St Peter's Church in 1966. St Peter's Street runs across the centre of the picture. Star Lane now carries traffic past the far side of the church from the double roundabout system, which is now in front of the Novotel Hotel. In the foreground is College Street. St Peter's Church, with its 93 foot tower, stands close to where Cardinal Wolsey founded his college. The Greyfriars development is being constructed in the background.

Before new defences were built, the River Orwell would often flood the area around Stoke Bridge during very high tides. This photograph was taken from a silo at the dock in September 1969 as the rail yards beside Commercial Road (now Grafton Way) and the dock quay were flooded. The building in the centre belonged to yeast manufacturers, British Fermentation Products Limited. A skateboard park has since been built on this site.

Barges loaded with grain sailing through the lock in 1955. Barges were a familiar sight at the dock with both Cranfield Brothers Limited (flour millers) and R & W Paul Limited (maltsters) running their own fleets. The town's gas works are visible behind the masts of the barges.

Top: The port area from over Greenwich in August 1968. New Cut and the dock are in the centre with the gas works centre right. Landseer Road is in the bottom right corner.

Bottom: An aerial view of the Ipswich port from above Cliff Quay in 1966. The engineering works of Ransome and Rapier is on the left bank. The remains of the Stoke Bathing building lie on the mud flats where the West Bank Terminal is now located. The dock is top centre.

The dock from one of the gas holders at the gas works in February 1958. Beyond the coal store of the gas works is the engineering works of Ransomes Sims and Jefferies who produced mainly agricultural machinery. The company moved from the site through the 1960s to a new works on the edge of town on the Nacton Road. The area has been transformed largely from commercial use to leisure, with flats and restaurants occupying much of the quay. It is now known as The Waterfront.

The Cobbold Brewery at Cliff Quay in the late 1950s. Beer was brewed on this site from 1746. Water was taken from the Holywells estate where it ran to the River Orwell. This building was constructed between 1894 and 1896. In 1957 Cobbold's merged with the Tollemache brewery, which was located between Tacket Street and Carr Street. All brewing had moved to this site by 1961, where it continued until production ceased completely in 2002.

Thames barges on the River Orwell near the dock lock gates in December 1955. The West Bank Terminal is now on the right of this view.

August 1960. A diver prepares to enter the water in the lock for maintenance work at the dock. The original lock off New Cut, then the largest in the country, opened in 1842, three years after the first stone was laid in a ceremony in 1839. The Wet Dock opened in 1842. The present lock opened in 1881 solving the problem of ships turning from New Cut into the lock.

The barge Venture in the dock in July 1956. This photograph was taken near the lock looking towards the town.

The barge Kimberley moored at the Stoke Bridge end of the dock in August 1967. The mills of Cranfield Brothers seen in the background were redeveloped in 2006 into flats and a dance studio.

The fire brigade were called to the dock in May 1965 to deal with a blaze at Neptune Quay. The former maltings of the Friary Meux Company were in the process of being demolished. Flats overlooking The Waterfront are now on this site. The silo in the background, close to Coprolite Street, belonged to Eastern Counties Farmers.

The opposite view of Neptune Quay taken from near Coprolite Street in May 1964.

St Helen's Street from Grimwade Street in the 1950s. All of these shops up to Wells Street were demolished and Wells Court flats built on the site. The shops from the left include G. Deeks estate agents, Frederick Ansell radio engineer, King and Waters opticians, S. Ilott grocers, R Bartlett hairdressers, and Fairfax Limited dyers and cleaners.

One of the shops demolished in St Helen's Street was Mrs Minter's "Open All Hours" business which sold everything from cough sweets to soup. Mrs Minter was known to her customers as 'Ma Minter'. The shop later moved to Grimwade Street.

Fore Street from Salthouse Street in 1961. This was then the main route to and from the east side of town. On the left is Herbert Wells butcher's shop.

Fore Street in 1961 with Fore Street Baths in the centre. The baths opened in 1894 in one of the poorest parts of Ipswich, the St Clement's area, and provided the town with its very first heated pool. The shops on the left were demolished and traffic diverted through here from Salthouse Street before Star Lane was cut through to Grimwade Street. The shops pictured here on the left include Weston's Limited, the television and radio dealers, and The Record Collectors' Shop.

Crowds lined Fore Street in 1961 for the Queen's visit to town. The crowd is standing opposite Grimwade Street. The buildings behind the crowd have since been knocked down and replaced by flats.

Shops on Fore Street from the direction of Grimwade Street. The buildings featured in the picture, now demolished, were, from left to right: C.H. Healey (stationer and post office), Meux's Brewery Company Limited and Mellonie and Goulder Limited (coal coke and salt merchants).

Workmen from J. Howard demolition contractors of Ipswich dismantle the last windmill in Ipswich in the early Fifties. The mill stood in Tower Mill Road between Bramford Road and the River Gipping.

The Piper's Vale swimming pool on the east bank of the River Orwell was built in 1937 between the new Gainsborough council housing estate and the river. On warm days the pool was packed with swimmers enjoying the facility. The view down river was to open countryside where the Orwell Bridge is today. The view towards town was not quite as picturesque, however, overlooking the Cliff Quay power station and sewage works. The pool was demolished in 1979 when a temporary road was cut through the site for the construction of the Orwell Bridge.

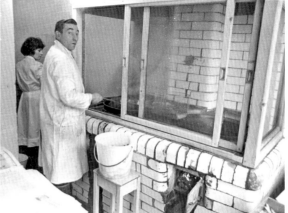

Top left: Children help an RAC man get his motor cycle and sidecar up Woodbridge Road hill after a fall of snow in February 1962.

Top right: One of the town's legendary fish and chip shops, Sabbatella's in Orford Street, where the fat was heated by coal fires. This popular shop would see queues all the way along the street on frying days.

Above: Crowds in typical 1950s clothing pose for the camera around a market fruit stall opposite the Royal William public house in London Road.

Top left: The fire station in Bond Street in 1951. Horse-drawn steam powered water pumps operated from here until the first motorised vehicle arrived around 1918. Bond Street was the town's fire headquarters until it relocated to Colchester Road, later moving on to the new station in Princes Street.

Top right: Floodlighting illuminated Cliff Quay power station for the Coronation celebrations of 1953. The station was badly damaged by fire in September 1982, signalling the end of power generation at Cliff Quay. The station was demolished in 1994, with thousands watching from every vantage point as explosives brought down the three chimneys.

Above: The mansion on Holywells Park was built around 1814 by John Cobbold as his family home. He used the water from Holywells for his brewery at the nearby Cliff Quay. The estate was presented to the town by Lord Woodbridge in the 1920s, but demolished in 1962. The stable block and clock tower are all that remain today.

Tyler Street around 1960. The Stoke area of town was packed with streets of small terraced houses. The Victorian houses were built as hundreds left the countryside to take work in town at the huge engineering works nearby. The houses on the left of this view have since been demolished and the Wherstead Road bypass now cuts through here.

The junction of Felaw Street (right) and Great Whip Street from Wherstead Road. On the right is Haward's bakery. The Wherstead Road bypass cuts across the foreground of this view today.

The low lying areas of Ipswich were hit by the East coast floods, which had struck during the night of Saturday, January 31, 1953. That day, strong winds drove a storm tide surge down the North Sea and by evening this had reached the east coast where sea defences were damaged by the huge waves. Breaches occurred in 1,200 places resulting in disastrous floods. It was one of the worst peacetime disasters ever known. 307 people lost their lives, 24,000 homes were damaged or destroyed, and more than 30,000 people had to leave their homes. Canvey Island in Essex, with a population of over 11,000, was worst hit; the whole island was submerged under water and 58 people died. At Felixstowe hundreds were made homeless and 40 people lost their lives. The Stoke area of Ipswich suffered badly as the River Orwell flooded homes and factories. This was taken in Bath Street during the clear up operation.

There was so little traffic in the town in the early Fifties that children were able to play in the street. This view of Station Street is looking towards Wherstead Road. Webb Street is off to the right with C. Jennings' bakers shop on the corner.

Transport

Public transport in the 1950s and '60s was often cold and a bit grubby, but is remembered with great affection. Until they were taken out of service in August 1963, the main bus routes in town were by trolley bus.

These quiet, pollution-free buses or 'trackless trams' replaced the regular trams, which had run on the same routes set out when the service came into use in 1903. The trolleys ran from the Constantine Road and Cobham Road depots.

At peak times, the only chance of getting one from the town centre was to board at Tower Ramparts, as they would be full from there giving no chance of boarding en route.

An open door at the rear and some with hard wooden seats brought little comfort on the journey on a cold day.

The overhead cables and power pick up arms would spark on frosty days. The arms would often come off the lines and the conductor would pull a long pole from the side of the bus to reconnect the supply. For all their problems, the people of Ipswich loved the trolley buses.

The last great decade for steam trains was the 1950s. Like the buses, diesel power was taking over. Huge clouds of smoke and steam would fill the air as locomotives pulled carriages and trucks along. Relatively few commuted to London for work in those days, but holidays and days out often started with a ride on a steam train.

Few families had a car and many took the train to Felixstowe for days trips. Those waiting at Westerfield and Derby Road station would see trains arrive already full of excited parents and children on sunny summer days. Special services often had to be put on to cope with the demand.

A pair of trolley buses enters the Tower Ramparts bus station in the snow of February 1958. The building in the background was a showroom for Egerton's garage.

Protesting members of the Campaign for Nuclear Disarmament pass by the Tower Ramparts bus station, Crown Street, in September 1959. They were demonstrating for the closure of the American Air Force base, Bentwaters, at Rendlesham. The bus station now also occupies the car park area.

This trolley bus skidded and overturned as it travelled down Bishop's Hill during a torrential downpour in June 1955. All of the houses on the right have since been demolished.

Problems at the top of Bishop's Hill when this trolley bus, on the number two service to Priory Heath, rolled back into a coach pushing it into another trolley bus on the hill.

The trolley buses had a crew of two, a driver and conductor. As well as collecting fares the conductor would use a long pole, stored in an opening along the bus, to reconnect the bus to the overhead power lines if it became disconnected. This conductor was using a new style ticket machine on this service in August 1951.

Travelling from the Cornhill to Bourne Bridge, this trolley bus struck the front of the Crown public house at the junction of Bridge Street and Greyfriars Road in June 1953.

In September 1955, this Ipswich trolley bus, number 44, started its journey from the depot in Cobham Road, where the Ipswich Transport Museum is now located, to a London Museum. This picture was taken shortly before a Pickford's towing truck took the bus on its journey down the A12.

Fallen branches from a tree, near the Whitton terminus in Norwich Road brought the number 113 service to a halt in the 1950s while the lines were cleared.

A British Railway Standard Class 7MT Pacific locomotive at the Station in 1951. This was number 7000, 'The Britannia'. Crowds gathered as the first haulage of 'The Norfolkman' arrived at the platform. The locomotive cut the time from Liverpool Street Station to Ipswich to one hour and fifteen minutes.

Steam locomotive number 61507 pulling coaches on the main Ipswich to London line.

Ipswich Station from near the tunnel on the main line to London. The siding on the right has been removed.

A view from the London Road bridge looking towards Hadleigh Road in the 1950s. The locomotive in the foreground is number 64724.

Locomotive number 67708 travels the Spring Road viaduct on the Felixstowe to Westerfield line in the 1950s.

The Flying Scotsman attracted many steam enthusiasts to the station when it pulled the Cathedrals Express in 1967.

Football & Speedway

Two teams represent Ipswich nationally in professional sport, Ipswich Town Football Club and Ipswich Speedway. The name of the town is well represented in both sports.

The football club saw huge changes during the 1950s and '60s. The club had turned professional in 1936, and in the early Fifties were playing in Division Three (South) of the Football League to crowds of around 10,000 at Portman Road. The team won that division in the 1953-54 season and were promoted to Division Two under manager A. Scott-Duncan. A disappointing season followed and the club was back in the lower league for the 1955-56 season.

Few would have predicted the events to come when Alf Ramsey took over as manager for the 1956-57 season. That season, they won Division Three (South), but sprang to prominence by winning the Second Division title in 1960-61. The following season, the "Cinderella club" astounded everyone by winning the Division One championship.

The town was wild with excitement for the club. The town centre was packed to capacity to greet their heroes for the civic reception at the Town Hall.

The club was relegated at the end of the 1963-64 season, but there was more celebration to come as manager Bill McGarry took the club back into Division One in 1968.

January 1969 saw the arrival of new manager Bobby Robson. Again few could have predicted the glory days that were on the horizon.

Speedway came to Ipswich in 1951 when a stadium was built at Foxhall Heath. The timing of the promotion was perfect. The public were keen on spectacular events to attend in the gloomy decade that followed the Second World War and crowds of up to 20,000 regularly attended the Witches' matches. By the early 1960s regular racing had come to an end. It was 1969 before young promoters John Berry and Joe Thurley built a new track inside the old one, which had been surfaced for stock car racing, and the Witches were reborn.

The Ipswich team that was promoted in the 1953/54 season. This team also took the club to the fifth round of the FA Cup. The players (from the left standing) are: W. Reed, J. Feeney, T. Garneys, J. Parry, G. McLucky, J. Elsworthy, and D. Rees. Front row: A. Scott Duncan (manager), B. Acres, A. Crowe, T. Parker, N. Myles, T. Brown and J. Forsyth (trainer).

The Mayor of Ipswich, Dr P. Weiner (left), held a reception at the Town Hall for the Ipswich Town team who won the Division Three (South) championship in the 1956/57 season. Manager Alf Ramsey (second left) stands with, from the left: Neil Myles, Ted Phillips, Roy Bailey, Billy Reed, John Elsworthy, Dai Rees, Ken Malcolm, Tom Garneys, Jimmy Leadbetter, Basil Acres, and club chairman John Cobbold.

Club trainer Jimmy Forsyth (right) with a group of players in the early 1950s. They are from left to right: Tommy Parker (captain) Dai Rees, Jim Feeney, Neil Myles, Basil Acres and goalkeeper Jack Parry.

Action from Portman Road in the 1950s. John Elsworthy is running with the ball on the right. This photograph was taken from the Churchman's stand end.

Spectators at Portman Road had little protection from the weather in the 1950s. The crowd in the background of this action shot have the practice pitch behind them. The large chimney visible behind the crowd is from the Constantine Road power station and trolley bus depot. It was used as an incinerator at the depot to burn some of the town's rubbish until it was demolished in 1958.

There were no flash cars and suits for the Ipswich Town players in the 1950s. They either travelled by bus, cycled or walked to the Portman Road ground for match days and were frequent visitors to Jimmy's Café in Princes Street for a meal after training. This group of players were walking near the ground in the early 1950s. They are (from left) Jack Parry, Joe Ball, David Deacon, Basil Acres, John Elsworthy, Jim Feeney, Vic Snell, Tommy Brown, Dai Rees, Neil Myles and Willie Jones.

An old cricket pavilion doubled as the changing rooms and offices at Portman Road until the mid 1960s. Pictured here standing in the pavilion in the 1950s, are (from left) Basil Acres, Joe Ball, Jack Parry, Tommy Brown and trainer, Jimmy Forsyth.

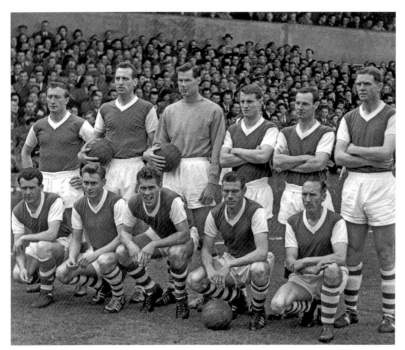

When Ipswich Town Football Club won the Second Division Championship in the 1960-61 season, nobody thought they stood a chance of staying in the top flight for more than one season. So the club surprised everybody by winning the league championship on April 28, 1962. In the final match of the season at Portman Road they defeated Aston Villa 2-0 while Chelsea, who were already relegated, went to Burnley and held them to a draw. The championship team pictured here was (from the left standing): Larry Carberry, Andy Nelson (captain), Roy Bailey, Billy Baxter, John Compton and John Elsworthy. Front row: Roy Stephenson, Doug Moran, Ray Crawford, Ted Phillips and Jimmy Leadbetter.

The goalkeeper stretches as Ray Crawford (out of shot) heads a goal direct from a Roy Stephenson corner in the game against Fulham. Crawford scored both of the team's goals in the match, but Ipswich lost 4-2 in front of 23,050 fans.

It was a historic moment for the "Cinderella Club" as Ray Crawford dived to score the first of two goals in the final match of the 1961-62 season against Aston Villa after team-mate John Elsworthy's header hit the bar. This was one of the most famous goals in the history of the club.

The crowd cheered with excitement when the team won the final match of the 1961-62 season to take the Division One league title. This picture of the Churchman's stand shows a great mixture of generations.

Championship celebration at Portman Road in April 1962. Getting a ducking in the communal bath is trainer Jimmy Forsyth. The players are (from the left) Jimmy Leadbetter, Roy Bailey, Ted Phillips, Larry Carberry, Ray Crawford and Andy Nelson the team captain.

The Cornhill was packed as the team arrived at the Town Hall for a civic reception in May 1962.

The team and club officials line up on the Cornhill before going into the Town Hall for a civic reception. Holding the trophy is team captain Andy Nelson.

Police officers hold back the excited crowd at the end of Tavern Street during the Ipswich Town championship celebrations of May 1962.

John Elsworthy and Jimmy Forsyth hold the Division One trophy aloft on the balcony of the Town Hall.

Manager Alf Ramsey with the Mayor of Ipswich, Charlotte Green, at the Civic Reception.

Just two seasons after winning the league, Ipswich Town dropped from the First Division at the end of the 1963/64 season having finished at the bottom of the league under manager Jackie Milburn. Bill McGarry took over as manager during the 1964/65 season, successfully taking the team to the top of the Second Division at the end of the '67/68 season. To celebrate, the team were paraded through town on an open top bus before attending a civic reception at the Town Hall. On the bus were team members and officials including club chairman John Cobbold, manager Bill McGarry, team coach Sammy Chung, Bobby Hunt, Colin Harper, Mick McNeil, Cyril Lea, Billy Baxter, Ken Hancock, Ray Crawford, Danny Hegan, Tommy Caroll, Frank Brogan, John O'Rourke, Ron Wigg, Derek Jefferson and Billy Houghton. In November 1968, Bill McGarry announced he was leaving the club to join Wolverhampton.

Bobby Robson was not the first choice to replace Bill McGarry. Ipswich initially went for Frank O'Farrell and Billy Bingham. Both declined, so Bobby Robson was recommended to the club by Dave Sexton, then the manager of Chelsea. It was the dawn of one of the club's greatest eras when Bobby Robson arrived at Ipswich Station in 1969. He was met by Ipswich chairman John Cobbold. With them is Mr Cobbold's chauffeur Roger Nightingale. After an unsteady start, the new manager took the club to triumph, winning the FA Cup in 1978 and the UEFA Cup in 1981.

Speedway came to Ipswich in 1951 when a stadium was built on Foxhall Heath. The first meeting was scheduled for Easter Saturday, March 24, but as thousands headed for the stadium the heavens opened and the track was covered in snow, which later melted and flooded the circuit. Here, riders line up at the start gate, which then had a concrete base, at the first meeting against Yarmouth. Riders (from the left) are: Billy Lamont (Ipswich), Johnny White, Rod Laudrum (Ipswich) and Fred Brand.

Huge crowds attended the meetings at Foxhall in the 1950s. Attendance figures regularly reached 20,000. This meeting against Yarmouth Bloaters in 1953 shows Johnnie Chamberlain, Harold McNaughton (Ipswich) and 'Titch' Read racing away from the starting line.

First bend action from June 1954 with Witches' Sid Clarke (left) and Len Silver racing K. Adams and B. Hanham (right) of Southampton.

The Witches' line up for the 1954 season. Back row (from left): 'Nobby' Stock, Len Silver, Dennis Day, John Lawrie. Middle row: Arthur Franklyn the team manager, Bert Edwards, Reg Reeves, Bob Sharpe, Dick Campbell, 'Junior' Bainbridge, Alex Moseley (mechanic), Charlie Frenzel (assistant team manager). Front row: Johnnie Chamberlain, Sid Clarke (team captain) and 'Titch' Read.

One of the most popular riders from the '50s era was 'Titch' Read. This spectacular crash occurred when he hit the bike of a fallen rider. The impact bent the bike's forks back. The photograph was captured by stadium photographer Don Harris on a plate camera, long before the days of motor driven cameras.

'Titch' Read on the centre green at Foxhall.

The Speedway team for 1962 (from the left standing) Vic Gooden (co-promoter), Colin Goody, Peter Moore, Sandy McGillivray, Maurice Littlechild (team manager), Bengt Brannefors, Leif Larsson, Les McGillivray and Eric Bason (co-promoter). Team captain 'Split' Waterman is on the bike at the front. This was the last season for the Ipswich team at Foxhall until a new promotion started in 1969.

Jack Unstead, who was killed at Foxhall stadium on April 13, 1962, while riding for the Witches. He hit the back wheel of another rider which sent him headlong into a floodlighting post.

Stock car racing continued at Foxhall Stadium after speedway racing came to an end. For several seasons the cars raced on the shale speedway surface before the track was surfaced. This spectacular crash was captured at the Easter race meeting of 1963.

Speedway returned to Foxhall in 1969 when promoters John Berry and Joe Thurley reformed the Witches, building a new, smaller track inside the old one which had since been surfaced for stock car racing. This was the team for a match against Crewe in August 1969. The riders are (from the left back row): Ron Bagley, Bernie Aldridge, Neville Slee and John Harrhy. Front row: Ted Spittles, Pete Bailey and Ernie Baker.

Music & Dance

Ballroom dancing was a popular social event during the 1950s. Among the popular venues were The Savoy in St Nicholas Street, The Arlington Ballroom in Museum Street and Victor Sylvester's Studio on the first floor at the Gaumont Theatre.

The 'baby boomer' generation were encouraged to learn to dance the waltz, quick step and tango by their parents. Ballroom dancing was the way thousands of couples met and socialised up to the early Sixties, with most teenagers taking lessons.

With the arrival of rock and roll and bands like The Beatles and The Rolling Stones, the trend for formal dancing came to an end and at the weekends hundreds of young people went to Victor Sylvester's studio to dance to pop records in a time before the word 'disco' had been thought up.

Many attended the live music of Bluesville at the St Matthew's Baths Hall and Manor Ballroom, more to listen to the top name bands than dance.

The local bands that Ipswich enjoyed were of a very high standard. Young people in the 1960s did not want to listen to traditional dance bands and instead followed the local bands that played rock, pop, and rhythm and blues. Many of the musicians appeared in several line-ups as the 1960s progressed.

Ipswich was on the map for national tours with all the top names coming to town. Rock and pop shows at the Gaumont included names like Buddy Holly, Little Richard, Roy Orbison, The Rolling Stones and The Beatles.

The BBC did not cater for the musical taste of teenagers during the explosion of rock and pop in the early Sixties. The arrival of pirate station, Radio Caroline, off Felixstowe in March 1964 meant Ipswich received a very powerful signal from the ship giving the station and the others that followed a huge young audience in town. When the government outlawed the stations in August 1967, fans greeted Caroline's defiant DJs Johnnie Walker and Robbie Dale at Ipswich Station as they headed back to the ship to become outlaws.

A popular dance hall in the 1950s and '60s was the Victor Sylvester Dance Studio at the Gaumont Theatre (now the Regent). 'Vicks' was always packed with teens and twenties at the weekend with a queue forming early to make sure of a place. The studio was run by Bob Morley and Rita Carlton. During the week they taught ballroom dancing, but at the weekend it was party time.

Rita Carlton and Bob Morley show the way at 'Vicks' around 1960.

In the early Sixties less formal dancing was the trend with dances like 'The Twist' taking over from the Waltz and the Tango.

A typical Saturday night at Victor Sylvester's in February 1964 as a packed crowd dance along to the popular records of the day.

The Hippodrome Theatre in St Nicholas Street opened in 1905 as a variety and music hall. In 1957 all the seating was removed and it was converted into the Savoy Ballroom where there was ballroom dancing on Saturday evenings and live rock and pop bands on Monday evening. These photographs were taken in February 1964; a time when the standard dress code was more formal for ballroom dancing.

Legendary live music promoters Ron and Nanda Lesley. This London couple brought Jazz and Blues to town for around fifteen years from 1958. They started with the Jazz Club. They also promoted a similar club in London and had close links with top musicians and promoters. In 1963 Ron Lesley started to introduce British rhythm and blues and the club evolved into Bluesville. They booked top names to appear in London at the weekend and Ipswich on a Monday evening. In the winter months gigs were at St Matthew's Baths Hall, with its famous bouncing floor covering the swimming pool. During the summer, when the pool was open, they moved Bluesville to the Manor Ballroom.

Among the acts Ipswich fans saw for a few shillings were, The Steam Packet with Julie Driscoll, Long John Baldry and Rod Stewart backed by Brian Auger, John Mayall's Bluesbreakers, Cream, Georgie Fame, the Yardbirds, and the Move. In 1971 they brought Led Zeppelin to the Baths Hall for £1 a ticket.

The 'Ready Steady Go' dancers on stage with Jimmy James and the Vagabonds at 'Bluesville' in St Matthew's Baths Hall in October 1966.

The Move on Stage at St Matthew's Baths Hall in March 1968.

St Matthew's Baths Hall from Berners Street in the mid '60s. The building is now hidden by shops and offices.

Bluesville advertisements from 1966.

Ipswich had its own excellent line-up of young bands from the early 1960s. Nick and the Nomads built up a great following with their own brand of rhythm and blues. The band was formed in 1962 and was soon packing halls in and around Ipswich. After a month-long booking in Hamburg, Germany, in 1964, the band signed a deal with HMV Records and released a single, 'You're Nobody Till Somebody Loves You'. Unfortunately the big time eluded them and the band split later that year. Members (from the left standing) are: Dave Cutting (lead guitar), Ben Foster (bass), Roy Clover (rhythm guitar) and Ron West (drums). At the front is lead singer Nick Wymer.

A group of Nick and the Nomads fans at a gig at Castle Hill Community Centre as the band plays in the background.

The Pete Croft Blues Band in a publicity photograph at Ipswich dock in 1968. The band had a great reputation with its pure blues performances. This line-up (from the left) was Pete Croft, Johnny Roach, Phil Quinby and Paul Gill.

The Sullivan James Band formed in 1965 and always had a good following with their soul music. They released 'Goodbye Mr Chips' on the Parlaphone label. This photograph was taken at a band practice in February 1966. The line up (from the left) was: Dick Maun (baritone saxophone), Dick Mayhew (trombone), Ron West (drums), Neville Moles (bass), Mick Noller (lead guitar), with Mick Finbow, seated at the piano, and Dick Moles (aka Sullivan James) on vocals.

The Nite Sect played mostly rock covers and always attracted an enthusiastic crowd. This photograph was taken as singer Mal Brierley signed autographs for fans at a gig in the Corn Exchange in May 1965.

The Nite Sect on stage at the Corn Exchange in 1965. The line-up was Mal Brierley on vocals, Derek Barber on bass, Melvyn 'Sem' Seaborne on keyboards, Roger Clarke-Johnson on lead guitar and Ken Smith on drums.

Cool School formed around 1968. The band played a mixture of soul and classic hits. The line up (from the left) was: John MacRea (drums), Roger Clarke-Johnson (lead guitar), Jerry Hovell (bass), Nick Wymer (vocals) and 'Sem' Seaborne (keyboards).

Les Blues at Ipswich Dock in 1964 (from the left): Gerry Gillings, Morton Lewis, John Game, Geno Washington and 'Koll' Patterson. Geno Washington was then an American serviceman based at Bentwaters airbase, Rendlesham. After returning to America at the end of his service he came back to Britain to form the nationally famous Ram Jam Band. In the early Sixties Geno was a regular at gigs often persuading the band's singer to take a break so he could sing.

The Sonics formed in 1963. The line-up from this photo taken around 1965 was Jim Bobby, Mick Morley, Alex Shulver, Barry Dye, Sue Carey and Clive Frindle.

Singer 'Jock' Davies has fronted many local bands. This photograph from the mid '60s was of one of the first, 'The Lord Bernard's Baby Bash Band'. The band was Jock Davies, vocals, Robbie Robertson, drums, Martin Boatfield, bass, Brian Rudd, trumpet, Chris Outhwaite, guitar, Danny Pitcher and Bernie Western, saxophone.

The Consorts were an early Sixties line-up. At the back (from left) are Barry Dye, John Doe and Alan Root. Kneeling are, Roger Runnacles, Mike Durrant and Colin May.

Guitarist Paul Glazebrook was in several bands, one of which, Unit Four, is pictured here. Band members from left to right are: Morton Lewis, Paul Glazebrook, Gerry Gillings and John Game.

The Epics in 1965 with (from the left) John Mayhew, Paul Glazebrook, Dave Lingard and Tony Coe.

The Gaumont Theatre (now the Regent) was visited by most of the big name bands of the 1960s. The Beatles visited twice; the first was in May 1963 just after their first number one hit single, 'From Me to You'. On 31st October 1964 the band was back in town. When tickets went on sale in July the queue stretched from the theatre in both directions with fans waiting all along St Helens Street and St Margaret's Street and into Woodbridge Road. Two girls at the front were there for 72 hours.

The Beatles being interviewed by Anglia Television at the Gaumont in October 1964.

Paul and Barry Ryan and Paul Jones were on tour in Ipswich in 1966. They signed autographs for local fans in their dressing room.

In March 1964 the monopoly on broadcasting in Britain, held by the BBC, was broken when pirate radio station Radio Caroline came on the air off the coast of Suffolk. The BBC broadcast very little pop music and Caroline built up a massive audience of young people with the all-day pop music format. The station was soon joined by other pirate ships and the government passed a bill to force the stations off the air. The law came into force at midnight on August 13, 1967. Radio Caroline decided to defy the law and stay on the air. The DJs travelled from London to the ships via Ipswich Station and then by road to Felixstowe Dock and by tender to the ships. A large crowd gathered at the station to send off 'outlaws' Johnnie Walker (above) and Robbie Dale (below).

The Radio Caroline ship, Mi Amigo.

Events

In the 1950s and '60s events would attract large crowds. Parades, royal visits, and visiting celebrities were seen as a good reason to line the streets.

On Coronation Day in June 1953 it poured with rain but it did not stop thousands from enjoying the parade of floats through town, or put a stop to their street parties.

When the Queen came to town in July 1961 to officially open the Civic College she was greeted by thousands as she toured the town in warm summer sunshine.

Circuses with performing animals were regular visitors. The animals would arrive by train and be paraded through crowds as they made their way to either Christchurch Park or Ranelagh Road.

Gerry and the Pacemakers were in pantomime in Ipswich in January 1964. Any visit out of the theatre was with strict security because of the crowds they attracted.

When Jimmy Tarbuck came to town in 1966, to open a new restaurant in the Buttermarket, he was greeted like a rock star as police struggled to hold back the good-natured crowd in the Buttermarket. It was a similar scene when former Radio Caroline DJ Simon Dee, who had become a television star with the BBC, came to open a shop in St Matthew's Street in 1969.

The annual Co-op fete in Christchurch Park saw over 20,000 heading towards the event well into the 1960s. Also in that period there was huge support for events organised by works sports and social clubs. Company staff outings were usually a sell-out.

The Coronation Day of Queen Elizabeth II on 2nd June, 1953 was wet and cold but it didn't stop a huge crowd gathering in Westgate Street to watch a parade of floats.

This float, with a nautical theme, was passing Egerton's Garage in Crown Street.

A fancy dress line-up in Cavendish Street, 1953.

Residents of Turner Road enjoying a party to celebrate the Coronation.

The Coronation day party in Kelly Road.

Three cheers for the Queen from residents of Prospect Street, Sirdar Road, and Mason Street.

The Queen visited Ipswich on the 21st July 1961. This was the Cornhill as the Queen's car turned from Princes Street into Tavern Street at the Cornhill. Her Majesty was in town to formally open the new Civic College.

The Queen toured Portman Road football ground in an open Land Rover. The stadium was full of local school children and representatives of local organisations. Here the Queen is being introduced to dignitaries as delighted schoolgirls look on.

The Churchman's stand at Portman Road
was packed with school children for the
Queen's visit in July 1961.

Huge crowds gathered at the station in March 1953 to watch the arrival by train of Chipperfield's Circus. The animals were paraded through the town to promote the show. In the background is the Station Hotel at the corner of Princes Street and Burrell Road.

Elephants of a another visiting circus leaving Ipswich Station in the 1950s after arriving in town by train. Circuses used a site at the junction of London Road and Ranelagh Road or Christchurch Park during their stay. Circuses featuring performing animals are no longer permitted in the Ipswich borough boundary. The houses in Ranelagh Road (right background) were demolished around 1960.

Crowds watching circus animals being loaded after arriving at the station in the 1950s. The building in the background was at the corner of Princes Street and Ranelagh Road.

Crowds on the Princes Street bridge in March 1953 watching a circus parade as it leaves the station. In the background is The Station Hotel at the corner of Princes Street and Burrell Road.

Liverpool comedian Jimmy Tarbuck attracted a huge crowd in the Buttermarket when he came to town in May 1966 to open Limmers restaurant.

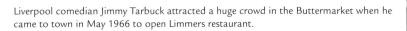

Smiling policemen help Jimmy Tarbuck through the crowd in the Buttermarket.

Jimmy cuts the tape to officially open Limmers in May 1966.

The Ambassador Bowling Alley was built on the site of a skating rink in London Road in the early 1960s. The sport was fashionable and thousands would queue for hours to get a lane for a game. In July 1963 the cast of a visiting show starring Rolf Harris joined locals for a match.

Rolf Harris signing autographs for fans at the Ambassador Bowling Alley in July 1963.

Gerry and the Pacemakers were appearing in the pantomime 'Babes in the Wood' at the Gaumont Theatre in January 1964. During their stay in town they visited Seaman's Dairy in Knightsdale Road, where Gerry sang to the ladies while the rest of the band helped the staff. The band had just become the first to have number one hits with their first three records, 'How Do You Do It?', 'I Like It' and 'You'll Never Walk Alone'.

The Co-op Fete was held annually in Christchurch Park. Thousands attended the event, which featured athletics, acrobats, boxing matches and political speeches. This picture of the funfair was taken in July 1966.

The Suffolk police force was split into three separate squads until 1967 when West, East and Ipswich Borough forces amalgamated to form one constabulary for the whole of the county. The Suffolk force headquarters was initially at County Hall in Ipswich, but eventually moved to Martlesham. The Ipswich police station remained at the Town Hall until the new borough station opened at the corner of Civic Drive and Elm Street.
The Ipswich Borough force held their annual inspection at the Ipswich Town Football Club ground at Portman Road.

A huge crowd filled Carr Street when Pat Phoenix, who played Elsie Tanner in Coronation Street, came to town in November 1965 to open a modernised part of the Co-op store.

Pat Phoenix signing an autograph for a fan.

Crowds lined Carr Street in October 1963 when yet another Coronation Street star, Peter Adamson, who played Len Fairclough, was at the Co-op store to open a new department.

An annual staff outing for Phillips and Pipers clothing factory in the early 1950s. Thousands of locals worked at the huge works between Old Foundry Road and St Margaret's Street, which closed in 1982 after a history spanning 131 years. The works building (background) has since been converted into flats at 'Pipers Court'.

The mainly female employees enjoy an annual outing. This photograph was taken as the group set off from Christchurch Works (background) for Windsor in July 1960.

May 1, 1960. Key Street was closed to traffic as a service was held to dedicate St Mary at the Quay Church as a new headquarters for the Boys' Brigade. In the background are the premises of Cranfield Brothers Ltd flour millers.

Television and radio star Simon Dee makes his way through a packed St Matthew's Street as he arrives to open a new Tesco store in March 1969.

School Days

The education system in Ipswich in the 1950s and '60s was quite clear-cut. Those who passed their eleven-plus went to Northgate Grammar School; for the rest it was a secondary modern school.

The only time the boys and girls of Landseer Road and Nacton Road met was at the annual sports day held on the sports field at Landseer School. These girls found some shelter from the rain at the event in June 1963.

Life at the town's secondary moderns came as a culture shock for those who had attended quiet, organised junior schools in smart uniforms.

It was tough at some of the schools. Discipline was often maintained by a whack with the cane, yet many from that generation have fond memories of the schools and their staff.

Some of the schools like Landseer and Tower Ramparts have since been demolished; others have expanded into sixth form colleges with pupils staying on into their late teens.

All a stark contrast from half a century ago, when boys and girls walked out of the school gate for the last time at 15 often with no qualifications. For most it was a case of stepping from school straight into the workplace where they were trained immediately in a specific trade or profession.

Landseer Secondary School for boys was built in the 1930s to serve the Gainsborough and Greenwich and Rivers Estates. Girls attended the Nacton Road Secondary School. The original quadrangle (right) was extended when the school became a mixed comprehensive. It has since been demolished and housing now stands on the site. The streets are named after long-serving teachers.

Pupils of Landseer Secondary School shelter from the rain at the annual school sports day in 1963.

The annual speech day at Nacton Road Secondary School for girls in July 1963.

Smart uniforms at the annual speech day at Chantry Secondary School in July 1963.

Tower Ramparts Secondary School was in the town centre, behind the spire of St Mary-le-Tower church. The Tower Ramparts Shopping centre now stands on this site. The White Horse Hotel, at the corner of Tavern Street and Northgate Street, is in the centre at the bottom of this aerial view.

The successful Tower Ramparts School football team of the 1950-51 season.

TOWER RAMPARTS, S.M. BOYS. IPSWICH.
ROCQUAINE BAY CAMP. GUERNSEY 1956.

School trips provide memories for the rest of our lives. This was the party of pupils and teachers from Tower Ramparts on a trip to Guernsey in 1956.

Teachers at Westbourne School in 1966. Names from the left include:
Front row: Mr Colmore, Mr Smith, Mr Laws, Mr Saunders, unknown, Mr Griggs, Mr Burley, unknown. Middle row: Unknown, Mr Ives, Mr Swan, Mr Greenacre, unknown, Mr Ward, Mr Newman, Mr Gillam, and Mr Danahar. Back row: Mr Hollis on the far right is the only identified teacher.

The annual junior school sports day was held on the main pitch at Ipswich Town Football Club until the late1960s. These boys are heading for the tape with the North Stand in the background.

The start of a girls' race on the pitch at Portman Road football ground in the mid Sixties.

Pupils cheer on their team at the junior school sports day at Portman Road in June 1966.

Christmas time for children is always a special occasion. These pupils took part in the nativity play at Chantry Junior School in the 1950s.

Christmas party time for a group of children whose parents worked for the East Anglian Daily Times Company in 1964. Almost every large company had an active sports and social club, which as well as organising sports and social events, would cater for children of school age. Sadly most of the town's sports and social clubs have now closed.